THE 12 WORST HURRICANES OF ALL TIME

by Susan E. Hamen

12 STORY LIBRARY

www.12StoryLibrary.com

12-Story Library is an imprint of Bookstaves.

Photographs ©:Harvepino/iStockphoto, cover, 1; BenjaminReilly/CC3.0, 4; Harry Koundakjian/Associated Press, 5; Library of Congress, 6; Library of Congress, 7; NOAA, 8; Rolfmueller/CC3.0, 8; PD, 9; NOAA, 10; Jocelyn Augustino/FEMA, 11; Gregory Bull/Associated Press, 12; Marco Ugarce/Associated Press, 13; Bob Epstein/FEMA, 14; Bob Epstein/FEMA, 15; Ed Rappaport/National Hurricane Center/NOAA, 15; NOAA, 16; Kyodo/Associated Press, 17; Josh Henderson/CC2.0, 18; Staff Sgt. James L. Harper Jr./US Air Force, 19; PvdV/CC3.0, 20; PvdV/CC3.0, 21; Master Sgt. Mark C. Olsen/US Air Force/New Jersey National Guard, 22; US Fish and Wildlife Service - Northeast Region, 23; Bonhams/PD, 24; Walter Hellebrand/CC3.0, 25; 1Lt. Zachary West/The National Guard, 26; Staff Sgt. Balinda O'Neal Dresel/US Army National Guard, 27; Henryk Sadura/Shutterstock.com, 28; Lisa F. Young/Shutterstock.com, 29; Koldunov Alexey/Shutterstock.com, 29

ISBN
978-1-63235-538-6 (hardcover)
978-1-63235-603-1 (paperback)
978-1-63235-657-4 (ebook)

Library of Congress Control Number: 2018946727

Printed in the United States of America
Mankato, MN
June 2018

About the Cover

Typhoon Nina approaching Taiwan in 1975.

Access free, up-to-date content on this topic plus a full digital version of this book. Scan the QR code on page 31 or use your school's login at 12StoryLibrary.com.

Table of Contents

1

Bhola Cyclone Batters Asia's Bay of Bengal

One of the worst storms in history struck Asia's Bay of Bengal on November 11, 1970. The Bhola Cyclone battered villages in present-day Bangladesh. Ocean waters rose 20–30 feet (6–9 m) above normal. Islands and low-lying coastlines were completely covered by water.

People in these areas fought to stay alive during the storm surge. Some climbed onto rooftops. Others scaled trees. There was no higher ground that people could flee to.

The powerful cyclone featured wind speeds over 140 miles per hour (225 km/h). Entire villages were wiped out. At least 300,000 people died, making the Bhola Cyclone one of the deadliest weather events in history.

The storm was so deadly in part because it struck at night. Many people were asleep when it hit. In addition, people did not receive any warning of the coming cyclone. Officials saw the storm on radar, but there was no way to share weather information. People in affected areas did not have televisions or radios to receive updates.

Track of the Great Bhola Cyclone

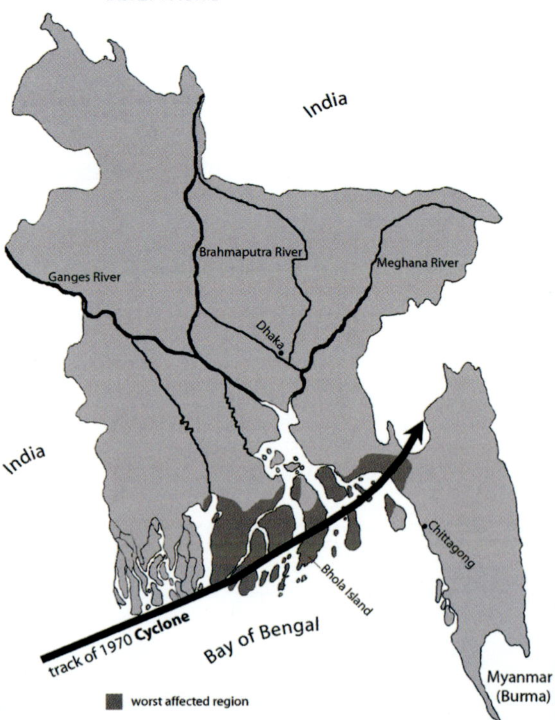

source: M.A. Samad, Cyclone of 1970 and Agricultural Rehabilitation

Low-lying coastline was devastated by the storm surge.

300

Number of countries that sent aid to cyclone victims.

- In 1970, the Bhola Cyclone devastated villages in present-day Bangladesh.
- People climbed onto roofs or up trees to escape the storm surge.
- The death toll was high because people had no warning of the storm.

HOW HURRICANES, TYPHOONS, AND CYCLONES ARE DIFFERENT

The terms hurricane, typhoon, and cyclone all describe a weather system of rotating storms. The terms are different because of where the storms begin. Storms forming in the North Atlantic, Northeast Pacific, and central North Pacific are called hurricanes. Northwest Pacific storms are known as typhoons. And storms in the South Pacific and Indian Ocean are called cyclones.

2

Great Galveston Hurricane Pounds Texas Coastline

Galveston, Texas, had sunny skies and light winds on September 7, 1900. There was no hint a terrible storm was on the way. The next day, a Category 4 hurricane hit the unprepared city.

Residents of Galveston had heard nothing about the storm. In 1900, there were no radio or TV stations. Telephones were very limited. Some information came in over telegraph wires. But news had to be printed in newspapers. When the hurricane hit, there was no time to warn any of Galveston's residents.

This entire neighborhood was reduced to piles of scrap wood.

The hurricane brought winds of over 135 miles per hour (217 km/h). Property not destroyed by wind was washed out by water. A 15-foot (4.6-m) surge of ocean water washed over Galveston and knocked buildings off their foundations. Structures were left as piles of scrap wood. More than 3,600 houses were completely demolished.

There was also a massive human toll. By the time the Great Galveston Hurricane blew out of town, it had killed an estimated 8,000 people. It is the deadliest natural disaster in US history.

ISOLATED BY DISASTER

Galveston sits on an island just off the coast of Texas. The hurricane destroyed bridges connecting Galveston to the mainland. It also destroyed all telegraph lines, cutting off the city. It took two days for messengers to reach Houston with news of the hurricane. They reported that approximately 500 people had died. The true scope of the destruction would not be known for weeks after.

$605 million

Amount of damage the hurricane caused in 2016 dollars.

- The residents of Galveston had no warning the hurricane was on its way.
- Winds exceeding 135 miles per hour (217 km/h) helped destroy the city.
- The Great Galveston Hurricane is the deadliest US natural disaster on record.

Survivors search for valuables in the wreckage.

3

Typhoon Nina Hits China's Henan Province

It is common for strong storms to develop in the Philippine Sea. August is one of the worst months for typhoons. The year 1975 was no exception. That's when Typhoon Nina blew in from the sea.

The storm made landfall in Taiwan on August 3. Winds of up to 138 miles per hour (222 km/h) battered the island. While some damage occurred, the strongest part of the typhoon was weakened by mountains in the central part of the country. This prevented even

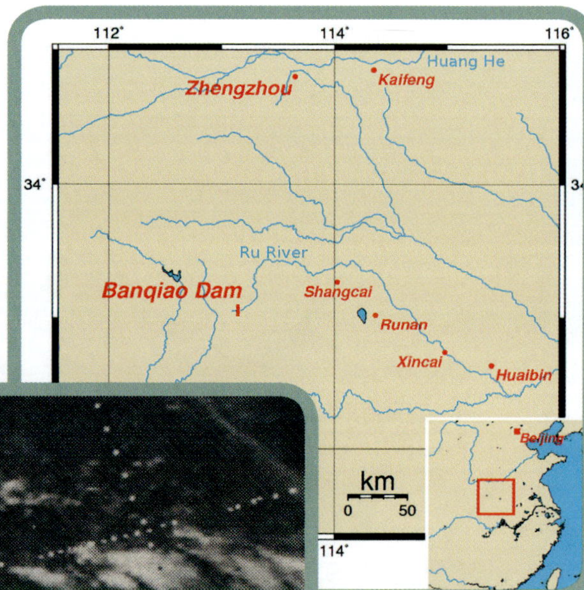

worse damage in Taiwan's most populated areas.

After hitting the island, Typhoon Nina crossed the Taiwan Strait to mainland China. Wind speeds dropped to 69 miles per hour (111 km/h). The storm was much weaker. The wind was not the biggest problem now. It was the rain. The rotating system stayed over the Chinese province of Henan for three days. During that time, nearly 64 inches (163 cm) of rain fell. Henan received more rain in 24 hours than the area normally received in an entire year. The Ru River swelled with floodwaters, putting pressure on the Banqiao Dam.

By August 9, the dam could no longer hold. A wall of water more than 10 feet (3 m) high and 6 miles (10 km) wide rushed downstream. Other dams failed. Roughly 160 billion gallons (600 cubic m) of water rushed through Henan Province. Many people could not escape. More than 220,000 people died from flooding caused by Typhoon Nina.

The Banqiao Dam could not hold back the Ru River floodwaters.

62

Dams that failed after Typhoon Nina.

- Strong storms often develop in the Philippine Sea.
- Typhoon Nina made landfall in Taiwan before continuing on to mainland China.
- The Chinese province of Henan was hardest hit by the storm.

4

Hurricane Katrina Slams into Gulf Coast

Hurricane Katrina first hit the United States on August 25, 2005. The Category 1 storm made landfall in southern Florida. It brought winds greater than 70 miles per hour (113 km/h) and several inches of rain before moving into the Gulf of Mexico.

In the gulf, the storm grew stronger. By August 27, Katrina was a massive Category 3 storm. It covered nearly all of the Gulf of Mexico, delivering winds that topped 170 miles per hour (275 km/h). Two days later, the storm made landfall. Beachfront buildings in Mississippi and Alabama were lashed by winds and flooded in the storm surge.

In New Orleans, Mayor Ray Nagin had already ordered an evacuation. There was great risk of flooding. Much of the city was below sea level. Only levees protected it from rising water.

Katrina brought heavy rains and a massive storm surge. The levees began to break. On August 29, about 20 percent of the city was flooded. By the next day, New Orleans was a disaster zone. Levees had continued to fail. Eighty percent

A satellite image shows how massive Hurricane Katrina was over the Gulf of Mexico.

of the city was underwater. People who had not evacuated were stranded in their homes or shelters in terrible conditions.

Hurricane Katrina was devastating across all of the areas it hit. More than 1,800 people are thought to have died. Storm costs reached $161 billion in 2017 dollars. The storm remains one of the deadliest and most expensive hurricanes in US history.

254,502

Population decline in New Orleans six years after Hurricane Katrina.

- Hurricane Katrina first hit Florida before growing stronger in the Gulf of Mexico.
- Alabama, Mississippi, and Louisiana had damage, with New Orleans worst hit.
- The hurricane remains among the deadliest and costliest US storms.

5

Mexican Paradise Turns Nightmare in Hurricane Pauline

Acapulco is a favorite vacation spot in Mexico. Tourists enjoy the tropical climate. They swim in the waters of the Pacific Ocean and play on the sandy beaches. But in October 1997, the tropical paradise turned into a nightmare. That is when Hurricane Pauline struck Acapulco.

The storm hit the area of Huatulco first. Homes were blown down. Fierce winds ripped through the area. Waves 30 feet (9 m) high crashed ashore. Water in nearby canals rose. Then it overflowed, sending 3 feet (1 m) of mud into the homes that were still standing.

The storm caused massive mudslides in the mountains behind Acapulco. Hundreds of cars, large trees, and boulders slid down the mountainside. People in the path of the mudslides were swept away. Many died. Flooding and mudslides ruined

The river near Huatulco overflowed its banks.

thousands of acres of crops and killed thousands of cattle.

Several hundred people died during Hurricane Pauline. Nearly 300,000 people were left homeless. Many also lacked food, water, clothing, blankets, or medicine. Other countries sent aid to help Mexico recover from the disaster.

130

Wind speeds reached in miles per hour (209 km/h) during Hurricane Pauline.

- Winds blew down homes and waves caused flooding in Acapulco.
- The storm caused mudslides that buried streets, homes, and cars.
- Nearly 300,000 Mexicans were left homeless.

THINK ABOUT IT

The World Meteorological Organization (WMO) keeps six lists of names for hurricanes. This way, they can use a different list every year for six years. After Hurricane Pauline, the WMO retired the name Pauline. They replaced it with the name Patricia. Why do you think they did this? Do some research to find out.

6

Hurricane Andrew Roars into South Florida

On August 24, 1992, Hurricane Andrew landed in South Florida. It was a Category 5 hurricane, which is the strongest and most destructive type. Andrew had pounded the Bahamas the day before. Wind speeds reached 175 miles per hour (282 km/h).

The hurricane crossed the Atlantic Ocean and hit Florida just south of Miami. The storm made landfall in the morning. Many people had sought safety in schools, community centers, and other government buildings opened as shelters. Those who hadn't hunkered down in their homes. Some took shelter in closets. They used mattresses to protect themselves from debris. Families huddled together as roofs blew off houses and walls crumbled around them.

Hurricane Andrew destroyed entire neighborhoods. In some areas, not a single home was standing. In others, the storm surge had flooded houses, leaving mud and debris behind.

High winds drove plywood through this palm tree in Homestead, Florida.

Cars and trucks lay where the winds had blown them. Trees were twisted over roadways.

Hurricane Andrew killed 65 people. It destroyed 63,000 homes and caused $26.5 billion in damage. Because it was such a destructive hurricane, the name Andrew has been retired. The World Meteorological Organization (WMO) will never use it for another Atlantic hurricane.

31

Schools destroyed by Hurricane Andrew.

- Hurricane Andrew's wind speeds reached 175 miles per hour (282 km/h).
- The storm caused $26.5 billion in damages and leveled many Florida neighborhoods.
- The hurricane name Andrew was retired.

THINK ABOUT IT

People in some areas were told to evacuate before Hurricane Andrew struck. Many did not. Why do you think these people stayed in their homes during the storm?

7

Japan Devastated by Super Typhoon Tip

Super Typhoon Tip is the largest storm ever recorded on Earth.

The Pacific Ocean has produced some major storms throughout history. But none has been as powerful as Super Typhoon Tip. A typhoon gets super status when it has wind speeds of at least 120 miles per hour (190 km/h). Super Typhoon Tip featured wind gusts of up to 190 mph (306 km/h). It is the most intense typhoon on record.

Super Typhoon Tip made landfall on the Japanese island of Honshu on October 19, 1979. The storm brought heavy rainfall and destructive winds. Bridges and buildings were destroyed. More than 600 mudslides were reported. And flooding cost many people their homes. Eighty-six people lost their lives.

The storm also hurt industry in Japan. Farmers lost their crops. Fishermen saw their boats sink. Some larger shipwrecks also occurred in the area.

Super Typhoon Tip is history's most intense typhoon. It is also the largest storm ever recorded on Earth. The typhoon measured approximately 1,380 miles (2,220 km) in diameter. This is the distance from Dallas, Texas, to New York City.

11,000

Number of people left homeless after Super Typhoon Tip.

- The storm caused flooding and mudslides on the Japanese island Honshu.
- Japanese industry was also impacted by the storm.
- Super Typhoon Tip is the most intense storm in history.

THINK ABOUT IT

What is the largest storm you have ever seen? What did you and your family do to stay safe? What might you do to be better prepared for future storms?

Over 600 mudslides occurred.

8 Texas Neighbors Wait Out Hurricane Ike

Early on the morning of September 13, 2008, Hurricane Ike tore into Galveston, Texas. The storm caused massive damage. The force of the winds brought a 20-foot (6-m) wall of water crashing down on beach homes. Some homes crumbled. Others were knocked loose. Survivors watched as entire houses floated by on the rising water.

People trapped in the hurricane called the National Guard for help. They were told it was too dangerous to try a rescue mission. They would

REFUSING TO LEAVE

The National Weather Service ordered people living in the Galveston area to evacuate. Many chose not to. In 2005, during Hurricane Rita, the Weather Service had ordered an evacuation. Huge traffic jams left people stuck on highways leading out of the city. About 90 people died of heatstroke and dehydration. People feared the same thing would happen again. They decided to stay put. Seventy-four people died when Hurricane Ike hit Texas.

View of storm surge in Galveston from a search and rescue helicopter.

have to wait out the storm. Many clung to hope for hours as they saw houses around them smashed to rubble.

People sought shelter in community centers and churches. As the hurricane winds blew outside, neighbors huddled together to stay safe from the storm.

Hurricane Ike is the third most destructive hurricane in US history. It caused $24 billion in damage in the United States and over $7 billion in Cuba.

30

Number of miles the storm waters pushed inland into Texas.

- Hurricane Ike hit Galveston, Texas, on September 13, 2008.
- A massive storm surge crushed homes and moved them off their foundations.
- People sought shelter in community centers and churches.

9

Many Jamaicans Left Homeless After Hurricane Gilbert

New Kingston, Jamaica, had clear blue skies on September 11, 1988. That night, young people danced at the city's clubs. Few worried about the weather. But out in the Caribbean Sea, a Category 3 hurricane was heading for the island nation.

The next morning, Hurricane Gilbert made landfall in Jamaica. Wind

50

Percent of drinkable water supply in Jamaica destroyed by the storm.

- The eye of the hurricane was 40 miles (64 km) wide.
- Property not damaged by winds was flooded by heavy rain.
- More than 300 people in eight countries died as a result of the storm.

This coconut grove was completely destroyed.

speeds reached 130 miles per hour (209 km/h). The center of the hurricane, called the eye, was 40 miles (64 km) wide. It covered nearly the entire island.

The monster storm destroyed buildings as it blew through. Most houses had tin roofs that were ripped off in the wind. Walls shook and crumbled. Homes not destroyed by wind were flooded. Thirty-two inches of rain fell. Crops were destroyed. Farm animals drowned.

Near the beach, tourists crammed into hotels for shelter. People waited in hallways, away from windows. They could hear patio doors and windows being ripped away. Many tourists had never seen a hurricane before. Some wondered if they would survive.

By the time Hurricane Gilbert moved past Jamaica, nearly 80 percent of homes were damaged or destroyed. Half a million people were left homeless. This was one-quarter of the population. Most of the island was without power.

Jamaica was not the only country affected by Hurricane Gilbert. The storm caused death and destruction across at least seven other countries. More than 300 lives were lost. The cost of the storm was more than $6 billion in 2017 dollars.

10

Hurricane Sandy Soaks Jersey Shore and New York City

The hurricane destroyed this pier along the New Jersey shore.

13.9

Storm surge level in New York's Battery Park in feet (4.2 m).

- People in New Jersey and New York were told to evacuate for Hurricane Sandy.
- Many chose not to leave and weathered the storm without electricity.
- Hurricane Sandy is among the costliest natural disasters in US history.

HURRICANE SANDY DISRUPTS ELECTION DAY

More than 600,000 people were still without power for the 2012 presidential election on November 6. Many polling stations were without power or underwater. Voters in these areas were allowed to vote in different ways. Some cast their votes at military trucks that were used as polling stations. Others emailed their votes.

Boats were left in piles at this marina after the storm.

People in the US states of New Jersey and New York watched the news closely in October 2012. Hurricane Sandy had barreled through Jamaica, Cuba, and Haiti. Now it was heading toward the East Coast of the United States.

Residents were warned to evacuate. But many chose to stay. People in the area had lived through Hurricane Irene the year before. Many who evacuated for that storm had little or no damage to their homes. As Hurricane Sandy approached, some thought it was not worth the trouble to leave.

Hurricane Sandy made landfall in New Jersey on October 28. It moved up the coast, hitting areas of New York City very hard. People watched as streets turned into rivers. Homes flooded. People with second stories spent the night upstairs to avoid the rising water. Many lost electricity and sat in the dark. Outside, cars and garages were underwater.

Hurricane Sandy destroyed 200,000 homes in all. Damage was estimated at $71 billion. It is among the costliest natural disasters in US history.

11 Great Hurricane of 1780 Ravages Caribbean Islands

In 1780, a violent hurricane made its way across the Caribbean Sea. Back then, hurricanes were not given human names, as they are today. This storm was called the Great Hurricane of 1780.

2

Houses left standing on the island of St. Lucia.

- Barbados, St. Lucia, and Martinique were hardest hit by the storm.
- An estimated 27,500 people are believed to have died.
- The Great Hurricane of 1780 is the deadliest Atlantic storm in history.

A painting by John Thomas Serres shows the wreck of the H.M.S. *Deal Castle* off Puerto Rico.

Foundations of coastal warehouses destroyed by the 1780 hurricane remain today.

Historians believe the hurricane formed on October 8, 1780. It started near the Cape Verde Islands off the coast of Africa. As the hurricane moved west across the Atlantic Ocean, it grew stronger and stronger. Barbados was the first island hit by the powerful storm. Wind speeds likely reached 200 miles per hour (322 km/h). Nearly every building on Barbados was destroyed.

Over the next two days, the hurricane passed over neighboring Caribbean islands. It brought great destruction to Martinique and St. Lucia. It slammed into Puerto Rico and the Dominican Republic. On October 18, it shifted course and headed north. The storm reached as far north as Newfoundland, Canada.

The Great Hurricane of 1780 killed about 4,500 people on Barbados. On St. Lucia, the death toll was estimated at 6,000. And on Martinique, approximately 9,000 people lost their lives. Historians believe the total number of fatalities across the eastern Caribbean reached about 27,500. The Great Hurricane of 1780 is the deadliest Atlantic Ocean storm in history.

12 Harvey Hits Texas with Hurricane Blast

It was August 2017. Officials at the National Hurricane Center watched a tropical storm in the Caribbean Sea. The officials were worried about the storm. If it got stronger, high-speed winds could cause destruction on the Texas coastline. Up to 50 inches of rain could fall. Parts of the state would get a year's worth of rain in just a few days.

Texas Governor Greg Abbott urged people in the hurricane's path to evacuate. Many left, but not everyone. Hurricane Harvey made landfall on August 25. It was a Category 4 storm with winds of 130 miles per hour (209 km/h). Along some coastal areas, as many as 80 percent of buildings were damaged or destroyed. Six hours of hurricane-force winds caused them to blow away or crumble.

In the city of Houston, heavy rainfall combined with Harvey's storm surge. The result was massive flooding.

A Texas National Guard soldier rescues a flood victim in Houston.

People who had stayed were in danger. Many waited for help on a second floor as floodwaters crept up the stairs.

Hurricane Harvey caused massive destruction. Nearly 300 miles of the Texas coastline was destroyed. More than 100 people lost their lives. A million more were left homeless.

$125 billion

Property losses from Hurricane Harvey.

- The hurricane formed in the Caribbean Sea before hitting Texas.
- Winds of 130 miles per hour (209 km/h) battered coastal areas.
- Massive flooding caused widespread destruction in Houston.

PET RESCUES FOLLOW HARVEY

Thousands of pets were rescued after Hurricane Harvey. Many were lost or left behind during the storm. Others were saved by their owners. But sometimes these people had no homes. They could not care for their animals. Pet rescue organizations helped find temporary and permanent homes for animals.

Staying Safe If There Is a Hurricane

- Evacuate the area if you can. If possible, families leaving by car should have a full tank of gas.

- Stay away from low-lying areas that will flood. It can become impossible to move to higher ground during a hurricane.

- Don't ride in a car through standing water. You can't tell how deep it is, and flooding may carry a vehicle away at any moment.

- Before a hurricane happens, work with your family to create a disaster plan. Know exactly where you'll go and who you'll be with if your home is damaged.

- Prepare an emergency kit that includes food, bottled drinking water, and medicines for those who need them. Pack at least a three-day supply of these items, along with life jackets, flashlights, and a battery-operated radio.

- Board up windows and doors that contain glass. Strong winds can send shattered glass flying through the air.

- Stay indoors in a secure spot. Stay away from windows or doorways. If possible, pull a mattress over yourself and family members to protect against flying debris.
- After a hurricane, stay indoors until you are notified it is safe to come out. There might be downed power lines and other dangers.
- Know how you will protect pets. Animals can get scared during storms. Plan in advance how you will keep them with you.

Glossary

canal
A human-made waterway that allows boats to travel inland from coastal areas.

category
A way to classify hurricanes by wind speed and how much damage they will do.

debris
Broken or loose material often appearing when something is destroyed.

dehydration
A medical condition that results when a person does not drink enough water.

evacuate
To leave a location, especially during a dangerous situation.

fatalities
Deaths occurring from disease or disaster.

heatstroke
A medical condition that occurs when a body is exposed to hot temperatures for a long time.

landfall
The location where a hurricane arrives on land after traveling across a body of water.

levee
A wall built to hold back rising water in rivers and other bodies of water.

polling station
A place people go to vote in an election.

storm surge
Water coming inland from an ocean or sea as the result of a storm.

tropical storm
A storm with strong winds, but not of hurricane intensity.

For More Information

Books

McAuliffe, Bill. *Hurricanes.* X-Books: Weather Series. Mankato, MN: Creative Education, 2017.

Carson, Mary Kay. *Inside Hurricanes.* Inside Series. New York: Sterling Publishing Company, 2010.

Royston, Angela. *The Science of Hurricanes.* Nature's Wrath: The Science Behind Natural Disasters Series. New York: Gareth Stevens Publishing, 2013.

Rustad, Martha E. H. *Hurricanes.* Little Scientist Series. North Mankato, MN: Capstone Press, 2014.

Index

About the Author

Susan E. Hamen has written more than 30 books for children on various topics including the Wright brothers, World War II, and ancient Rome. Hamen lives in Minnesota with her husband, daughter, and son.